The Ultimate Office 365 Guide: Tips & Tricks to Save Time & Use Office 365 Like a Pro

By Jon Albert

Copyright Info:

Legal Info:

This author and or rights owner(s) make no claims, promises, or guarantees in regards to the accuracy, completeness, or adequacy of the contents of this book, and expressly disclaims liability for errors and omissions in the contents within. This product is for reference use only. Please consult a professional before taking action on any of the contents found within.

Preface

We want to take a moment to say thank you for purchasing our guide online. HiddenStuff Entertainment remains one of the top app and eBook publishers online. It is our commitment to bring you the most important information to enrich your life.

We sincerely hope that you find this guide useful and beneficial in your quest for betterment. We want to provide readers with knowledge and build their skills to perform at the highest levels within their topics of interest. This in turn contributes to a positive and more enjoyable experience. After all, it is our belief that things in life are to be enjoyed as much as they possibly can be.

If you are in need of additional support or resources in regards to this guide, please feel free to visit our webpage at Hiddenstuffentertainment.com

Contents

Introduction

Office 365 tips

POWERPOINT DESIGN

Some years back, it took considerable time to have PowerPoint presentations. You are expected to select the backgrounds, layouts, fonts, as well as transitions. But with already existing templates, you can reduce the time you are using to look for backgrounds while maximizing the output of your content. Along with the customizable templates are design features that offer you suggestions regarding how you can arrange your slides after you've inserted an image. The moment a picture is inserted, a bar appears by the side to your left, with options on layout types, and choosing your slide is going to reflect your choice.

Image 0219: design

MORPH

It's a recent transition that lets you duplicate slides while you move about its components so they can look like they've shifted. This helps in creating something similar to gif by altering their location, rotation and sizes of the object. Then when the slideshow is played, you can witness the transition happening. For instance, these pumpkins appear like they've been thrown high and are undergoing some kind of spinning in the course of falling.

Image 0220: morph

TELL ME WHAT YOU WANT TO DO

This recent helpful functionality can aid you in finding and executing a couple of actions. Put pictures, have the document shared, include an excel chart, or print if you want. Close to its acrobat tab is a box. To implement it just put in some text and it will provide some suggestions depending on what you have entered to select from. For instance, if you wanted to have a checkbox inserted you would input and click "check box", it will be inserted for you. Perhaps, you need help on the said topic, you would find an option below that says "Get help on..."

Image 0221: tellmew

BING

Whenever you are searching or inserting pictures, you have the alternative of making use of Bing. That way, you have a better chance of doing stuffs the right way regarding the documents in contrast to launching another browser for searching your pictures or information. There are 2 options on how it can be done. One way is to right click as well as choose smart look up, or go proceed to "Tell me what you want to do box." You could find images, web search, define words, and look into Wikipedia.

Image 0218: bing

OUT USING CLUTTER, IN USING FOCUSED

Clutter is undergoing a replacement with an inbox that is more efficient. Already existing on outlook' mobile version, it will be available as a desktop version in no time, it functions by exploring what outlook considers as your relevant mails and those that are irrelevant which will be pushed onto the "other" section. It lets you manage a much neater inbox with only relevant emails to deal with. It equally allows scheduling of messages to go away from inbox while they can reappear at another time.

Image 0222: focused

INKED

Now existing in office' mobile version is a new tool known as "ink". It allows you to select colors from a certain color wheel while you can use them for drawing on your doc using a highlighter or pen. Choose draw tab from a ribbon that has four already set colors as well as color wheel. Doing your selection on the color wheel lets you move the tab about for finding a color. This allows for more flexible markups of your documents.

Image 0223: ink

THE TRINITY

Outlook now has three additional plugins. Sending of e-gift cards and scheduling of meetings with the Starbucks plugin. Implement its PayPal plugin for sending money securely to others through email. Or you can even place an order for Uber rides in connection with your calendar events, which will be sending you reminder for confirming your ride when the day comes.

Image 0224: paypal

Image 0225: starbucks

Image 0226: uber

BOOMERANG

Make the best of a smart calendar assistant which can assist you in scheduling meetings and sharing your availability through outlook. You can equally get reminders for following up on all emails that have not received any response and scheduling that your emails be sent out later.

Image 0227: boomerang

DELVE

An important aspect of Microsoft' business platform, this feature lets you monitor whatever is going on around you (on the condition that you can only see what you are privileged to). You can decide to click a colleague' name and view the document list that they have worked on in recent times, or even get a summarized display of every document that has been worked on by various persons, and with everything on the cloud, you could view the various versions that have been edited by these persons.

Image 0228: delve

PROJECT MANAGEMENT

Planner is for setting up a to-do-list for work groups. Set expected dates for task completion, collaborate, share files, and check on the dashboard for your team' progress. It's a nice tool for tracking milestones or goals that have been achieved by your group, and getting everyone on the same page.

Image 0229: planner

GROUPS

Having your team set up as one group for a certain project affords team members the privilege of sharing a space together. You would have the chance of sharing one inbox, group, and OneDrive folder on planner for setting up deadlines and goals. This is necessary for easy information transfer among members; there will not be any need to forward email to all team members when there is an update concerning changes in your project since everybody can access it.

Image 0230: groups

TAKE A POLL

With Sway you could create PowerPoints that are interactive, implementing videos and pictures for more interactivity. By integrating PollEverywhere.com to your presentations you could equally create poll for engaging your viewers and have them interact with whatever presentation you are doing.

Image 0231: poll

GIGJAM

This is a mobile sharing app that allows you to share snippets of Office 365 packages with other persons. Whether it is a photo or text it's fast and easy if you are not sending the whole document.

Image 0232: gigjam

COLLABORATING

Rather than have four persons work on one document and trying to put them all together, you can leverage Microsoft collaborative options. You can make your entire team edit a particular document while you can see every changes made real time. This will eliminate the problem of struggling to combine 3 or more different versions of that same document.

 Image 0233: collab

SKYPE AND EDIT

If you have Office 365, chances are that you have Skype for business for communicating with your colleagues. Office 365 provides you with two options regarding how you can use the various office products, the online or desktop version. The two options are acceptable for your using pleasure, although they've got various benefits. The online comes with auto syncing system, having your OneDrive directory, while the desktop provides you with the choice of saving on your hard drive even though that is not advised. It has equally introduced another stunning feature – collaborative editing. This lets you have a real time view of what others are editing. You can now chat on the document itself due a recent Skype plugin.

Image 0234: skypeedit

DATA MAPS

A recent feature on excel that can accept data in their rows and have them changed to a map. That means it changes anything you can imagine to images, organizes them in a country or state format depending on the available information. You could locate Power Map below Insert/Map tab which is inside your excel sheet.

Image 0235: map

Image 0236: maps

REFORMAT DATA IN A SNAP

This fill down command that is used by pressing control-D, which fills a row depending on the available information making the filling out of your spreadsheets much more productive. Flash fill in contrast will learn what you are doing and then reformat itself to look like it when you click on accept. Although this feature is not new, it is quite useful for those who use windows computer.

Image 0237: excel

MAKE THE UNREADABLE READABLE

Document scanning initially required a lot of effort and time, but now the Office Lense qualifies your smartphone as a reliable scanner, allowing you to take snapshots on the go. You can quickly have a picture snapped and see how it will be changed into a PDF, after which it will be uploaded unto your folder on OneDrive so it can be emailed to the parties involved. It equally takes illegible whiteboard texts as well as making it visible by making the image better, a necessary function that is needed for meetings. With these stored in the cloud, there would not be need for you moving around with physical papers; an absolutely green solution.

Conclusion

Once you start to implement the steps outlined you will be able to make a good presentation on PowerPoint. Good luck and enjoy!

CPSIA information can be obtained
at www.ICGtesting.com
Printed in the USA
LVHW021132150323
741658LV00023B/424